PERSONAL INFORMATION

Name:

Address:

Telephone: Email:

Employer:

Address:

Telephone: Email:

MEDICAL INFORMATION

Physician: Telephone:

Allergies:

Medications:

Blood Type:

Insurer:

IN CASE OF EMERGENCY, NOTIFY

Name:

Address:

Telephone: Relationship:

ISBN 978-1-63609-869-2

Published by Barbour Publishing, Inc., 1810 Barbour Drive, Uhrichsville, Ohio 44683, www.barbourbooks.com

Our mission is to inspire the world with the life-changing message of the Bible.

Member of the Evangelical Christian Publishers Association

Printed in China.

Pause and Pray

2025 Planner

BARBOUR
PUBLISHING

Pause. . .and Pray!

Devote yourselves to prayer,
being watchful and thankful.
COLOSSIANS 4:2 NIV

The all-powerful God cares deeply for you, even in the day-to-day details of your life. In fact, He longs to hear from you. You are invited—any time and for any reason—to bring any prayer to the King of the universe. Now that's genuine love!

The prayers in this lovely 17-month planner will help you develop a more intimate relationship with the heavenly Father. As you read the monthly and weekly devotional prayers, make them your own. Meditate on the scriptures.

You will be blessed all 365 days of 2025 when you pause and pray!

YEAR *at a* GLANCE

JANUARY

S	M	T	W	T	F	S
			1	2	3	4
5	6	7	8	9	10	11
12	13	14	15	16	17	18
19	20	21	22	23	24	25
26	27	28	29	30	31	

FEBRUARY

S	M	T	W	T	F	S
						1
2	3	4	5	6	7	8
9	10	11	12	13	14	15
16	17	18	19	20	21	22
23	24	25	26	27	28	

MAY

S	M	T	W	T	F	S
				1	2	3
4	5	6	7	8	9	10
11	12	13	14	15	16	17
18	19	20	21	22	23	24
25	26	27	28	29	30	31

JUNE

S	M	T	W	T	F	S
1	2	3	4	5	6	7
8	9	10	11	12	13	14
15	16	17	18	19	20	21
22	23	24	25	26	27	28
29	30					

SEPTEMBER

S	M	T	W	T	F	S
	1	2	3	4	5	6
7	8	9	10	11	12	13
14	15	16	17	18	19	20
21	22	23	24	25	26	27
28	29	30				

OCTOBER

S	M	T	W	T	F	S
			1	2	3	4
5	6	7	8	9	10	11
12	13	14	15	16	17	18
19	20	21	22	23	24	25
26	27	28	29	30	31	

2025

MARCH

S	M	T	W	T	F	S
						1
2	3	4	5	6	7	8
9	10	11	12	13	14	15
16	17	18	19	20	21	22
23	24	25	26	27	28	29
30	31					

APRIL

S	M	T	W	T	F	S
		1	2	3	4	5
6	7	8	9	10	11	12
13	14	15	16	17	18	19
20	21	22	23	24	25	26
27	28	29	30			

JULY

S	M	T	W	T	F	S
		1	2	3	4	5
6	7	8	9	10	11	12
13	14	15	16	17	18	19
20	21	22	23	24	25	26
27	28	29	30	31		

AUGUST

S	M	T	W	T	F	S
					1	2
3	4	5	6	7	8	9
10	11	12	13	14	15	16
17	18	19	20	21	22	23
24	25	26	27	28	29	30
31						

NOVEMBER

S	M	T	W	T	F	S
						1
2	3	4	5	6	7	8
9	10	11	12	13	14	15
16	17	18	19	20	21	22
23	24	25	26	27	28	29
30						

DECEMBER

S	M	T	W	T	F	S
	1	2	3	4	5	6
7	8	9	10	11	12	13
14	15	16	17	18	19	20
21	22	23	24	25	26	27
28	29	30	31			

AUGUST 2024

SUNDAY	MONDAY	TUESDAY	WEDNESDAY
28	29	30	31
4	5	6	7
11	12	13	14
18	19	20	21
25	26	27	28

THURSDAY	FRIDAY	SATURDAY
1	2	3
8	9	10
15	16	17
22	23	24
29	30	31

JULY

S	M	T	W	T	F	S
	1	2	3	4	5	6
7	8	9	10	11	12	13
14	15	16	17	18	19	20
21	22	23	24	25	26	27
28	29	30	31			

SEPTEMBER

S	M	T	W	T	F	S
1	2	3	4	5	6	7
8	9	10	11	12	13	14
15	16	17	18	19	20	21
22	23	24	25	26	27	28
29	30					

My Place of Quiet Peace

Lord, this world is so loud; it constantly shouts for my attention. My head fills up with so much stuff—things I need to do, questions I need to answer, and never-ending activity. The fast-paced merry-go-round of life won't stop, but I can step off. Help me remember to take time to slow down, to sit down and become quiet with You. Nowhere else do I experience the peace You provide. I need time with You every day. Help me to diligently spend those quiet moments with You. Let Your peaceful presence wash over me and quiet my soul.

GOALS *for this* MONTH

☐ ....

☐ ....

☐ ....

☐ ....

☐ ....

☐ ....

☐ ....

☐ ....

☐ ....

☐ ....

☐ ....

☐ ....

☐ ....

☐ ....

☐ ....

☐ ....

You're my place of quiet retreat;
I wait for your Word to renew me.

PSALM 119:114 MSG

Father, this morning I meet You here for just a few moments before the busyness of the day takes over. I trust You. It is not always easy to trust, but You have proven trustworthy in my life. I find joy in the knowledge that You are my defender. You go before me this day into battle. I choose joy today because I love the name of the Lord Almighty.

SUNDAY, July 28

MONDAY, July 29

TUESDAY, July 30

WEDNESDAY, July 31

THURSDAY, August 1

FRIDAY, August 2

SATURDAY, August 3

But let all those that put their trust in thee rejoice: let them ever shout for joy, because thou defendest them: let them also that love thy name be joyful in thee.

PSALM 5:11 KJV

Lord, You know it's hard for me to be still. I feel like I need to be doing something, but You have strongly encouraged me in Your Word to be still so that I might experience Your salvation. Help me rest in You. I open my heart and allow Your peace to comfort me. I will shut my mouth and listen as Your wisdom speaks to me. I stand in the quiet of Your presence and wait.

SUNDAY, August 4

MONDAY, August 5

TUESDAY, August 6

WEDNESDAY, August 7

THURSDAY, August 8

FRIDAY, August 9

SATURDAY, August 10

"The LORD is fighting for you! So be still!"

EXODUS 14:14 GW

Heavenly Father, I rejoice in my relationship with You. Today I offer the purest worship through thanksgiving. Thank You for the many undeserved blessings You bestow on me daily. You provide the air I breathe, the life I live, and the joy I experience. You hear my prayers always. I am grateful for Your presence; You are always near. I live my life today in absolute surrender to You.

SUNDAY, August 11

MONDAY, August 12

TUESDAY, August 13

WEDNESDAY, August 14

THURSDAY, August 15

FRIDAY, August 16

SATURDAY, August 17

Since we are receiving our rights to an unshakable kingdom we should be extremely thankful and offer God the purest worship that delights his heart as we lay down our lives in absolute surrender, filled with awe.

HEBREWS 12:28 TPT

Father, fill my heart with the absolute joy of Your presence today. Fill me with the peace of Your nature and the unwavering hope for my future. Everywhere I look, it seems I can always find a reason to doubt Your goodness and Your omnipotence. Forgive me for the way I have turned from You in moments of uncertainty. I choose, Lord, to start new and to see these complications as opportunities to trust in You.

SUNDAY, August 18

MONDAY, August 19

TUESDAY, August 20

WEDNESDAY, August 21

THURSDAY, August 22

FRIDAY, August 23

SATURDAY, August 24

May the God of hope fill you with all joy and peace as you trust in him, so that you may overflow with hope by the power of the Holy Spirit.

ROMANS 15:13 NIV

Because of what You've done, Jesus, my sins are forgiven and my transgressions are not counted against me. Through You, I am set apart. I have a hope and a future. I am considered righteous—but it's only through the glorious gift of God that I have a right standing with Him. And for this reason, I can live my life with confidence in You. I can stand solid in my faith, bold as a lion.

SUNDAY, August 25

MONDAY, August 26

TUESDAY, August 27

WEDNESDAY, August 28

THURSDAY, August 29

FRIDAY, August 30

SATURDAY, August 31

A wicked person flees when no one is chasing him, but righteous people are as bold as lions.

PROVERBS 28:1 GW

SEPTEMBER 2024

SUNDAY	MONDAY	TUESDAY	WEDNESDAY
1	2 *Labor Day*	3	4
8	9	10	11
15	16	17	18
22 *First Day of Autumn*	23	24	25
29	30	1	2

THURSDAY	FRIDAY	SATURDAY
5	6	7
12	13	14
19	20	21
26	27	28
3	4	5

AUGUST

S	M	T	W	T	F	S
				1	2	3
4	5	6	7	8	9	10
11	12	13	14	15	16	17
18	19	20	21	22	23	24
25	26	27	28	29	30	31

OCTOBER

S	M	T	W	T	F	S
		1	2	3	4	5
6	7	8	9	10	11	12
13	14	15	16	17	18	19
20	21	22	23	24	25	26
27	28	29	30	31		

Loving Others

Father, sometimes it's hard for me to love the difficult people in my life. They feel like a daily chore I add to my to-do list and check off, and not like a growing relationship. Sometimes we don't agree on the same issue, or they make drastically different decisions from my own. I feel like they never listen to me or respect my feelings. Lord, there are days when I don't believe they deserve my love and forgiveness.

Help me to understand that my ability to love grows from Your love that I am firmly planted in. It shouldn't be about me or what I'm feeling. I know that You forgave my sins on the cross and loved me in my difficult moments. Since this is true, I am confident that I have the ability to love others when it's hard, because it's a reflection of the love You already poured onto me.

GOALS *for this* MONTH

- [ ] ....
- [ ] ....
- [ ] ....
- [ ] ....
- [ ] ....
- [ ] ....
- [ ] ....
- [ ] ....
- [ ] ....
- [ ] ....
- [ ] ....
- [ ] ....
- [ ] ....
- [ ] ....
- [ ] ....
- [ ] ....

We love because he first loved us.

1 JOHN 4:19 NIV

Heavenly Father, I can be an emotional person. But even while acknowledging what is going on around me, I can still maintain my trust in You. I can be unshakable if I have established my dependence on You alone. I refuse to allow my circumstances to make me waver. I will remain cheerful no matter what, because my joy comes from You.

SUNDAY, September 1

MONDAY, September 2 *Labor Day*

TUESDAY, September 3

WEDNESDAY, September 4

THURSDAY, September 5

FRIDAY, September 6

SATURDAY, September 7

Be cheerful no matter what; pray all the time; thank God no matter what happens. This is the way God wants you who belong to Christ Jesus to live.

1 THESSALONIANS 5:16–18 MSG

Lord, I've cried out to You in my troubles so many times, I've lost count. Thank You for always being there. No matter the number of times I fall apart, You always comfort me in the middle of grief, loss, sorrow, or failure. You are my promise, and I cling tightly to You.

SUNDAY, September 8

MONDAY, September 9

TUESDAY, September 10

WEDNESDAY, September 11

THURSDAY, September 12

FRIDAY, September 13

SATURDAY, September 14

The L*ORD* *is close to the brokenhearted and saves those who are crushed in spirit.*

PSALM 34:18 NIV

Father God, help me remember when I read my Bible that Your Word gives me life. Your Word sustains me. And when I pray according to Your Word, all of heaven is backing me up. I rejoice in Your Word. As I go about my day, bring Your Word alive in me. Remind me of Your truth.

SUNDAY, September 15

MONDAY, September 16

TUESDAY, September 17

WEDNESDAY, September 18

THURSDAY, September 19

FRIDAY, September 20

SATURDAY, September 21

"Heaven and earth will pass away,
but my words will never pass away."

MATTHEW 24:35 NIV

Father, so many homes are shaken these days. So many families are shattering to pieces around me. Protect my home, I pray. Protect my loved ones. Be the foundation of my home, strong and solid, consistent and wise. May every decision made here reflect Your principles. May those who visit this home and encounter this family be keenly aware of our uniqueness, because we serve the one true and almighty God.

SUNDAY, September 22 *First Day of Autumn*

MONDAY, September 23

TUESDAY, September 24

WEDNESDAY, September 25

THURSDAY, September 26

FRIDAY, September 27

SATURDAY, September 28

Except the L*ORD* *build the house, they labour in vain that build it: except the* L*ORD* *keep the city, the watchman waketh but in vain.*

PSALM 127:1 KJV

Forgive me, Lord, for making obedience harder than it is. I feel like I'm unprepared for what You've asked me to do, but really, I have a hard time letting go. Give me courage to step out, trusting You'll provide everything I need to accomplish the task. You will give me wisdom to act and the words to speak. You will equip me. All I have to do is follow You.

SUNDAY, September 29

MONDAY, September 30

TUESDAY, October 1

WEDNESDAY, October 2

THURSDAY, October 3

FRIDAY, October 4

SATURDAY, October 5

The Spirit of the Sovereign LORD is on me, because the LORD has anointed me to proclaim good news to the poor. He has sent me to bind up the brokenhearted, to proclaim freedom for the captives and release from darkness for the prisoners.

ISAIAH 61:1 NIV

OCTOBER 2024

SUNDAY	MONDAY	TUESDAY	WEDNESDAY
29	30	1	2
6	7	8	9
13	14 *Columbus Day*	15	16
20	21	22	23
27	28	29	30

THURSDAY	FRIDAY	SATURDAY
3	4	5
10	11	12
17	18	19
24	25	26
31 *Halloween*	1	2

SEPTEMBER

S	M	T	W	T	F	S
1	2	3	4	5	6	7
8	9	10	11	12	13	14
15	16	17	18	19	20	21
22	23	24	25	26	27	28
29	30					

NOVEMBER

S	M	T	W	T	F	S
					1	2
3	4	5	6	7	8	9
10	11	12	13	14	15	16
17	18	19	20	21	22	23
24	25	26	27	28	29	30

Lord, I'm Tired

Lord, sometimes I feel like I don't have time to even breathe! My days are filled from the moment I wake up until the minute I go to bed. I tell myself I don't have time to rest because there is always one more thing to do, but You did not create Your children to live like this. On the seventh day of Creation, You rested. I can be positive that when I relax, I am not failing. I am preparing for the next task.

Teach me, God, to come to You when I'm tired and when I am overwhelmed. Only when I take the time to be in the presence of the Holy Spirit will I find myself truly refreshed, ready to take on what life has for me next. Help me to remember that You bring the greatest healing renewal.

GOALS *for this* MONTH

- [ ]
- [ ]
- [ ]
- [ ]
- [ ]
- [ ]
- [ ]
- [ ]
- [ ]
- [ ]
- [ ]
- [ ]
- [ ]
- [ ]
- [ ]
- [ ]

"Come to me, all you who are weary and burdened, and I will give you rest."

MATTHEW 11:28 NIV

Lord, I come to You today asking for peace in my family. Thank You for Your Spirit living in us and with us. No matter how much chaos is going on around us, we can rest and rely on You. Help us not to lose our composure when chaos erupts. Remind us to fix our minds and hearts on You. The world is filled with drama, but it doesn't have to be a part of our life. Help us keep Your peace as the center of our home.

SUNDAY, October 6

MONDAY, October 7

TUESDAY, October 8

WEDNESDAY, October 9

THURSDAY, October 10

FRIDAY, October 11

SATURDAY, October 12

And all your [spiritual] children shall be disciples [taught by the Lord and obedient to His will], and great shall be the peace and undisturbed composure of your children.

ISAIAH 54:13 AMPC

There are so many "how-to" books available today, Lord, and they all promise to increase my knowledge in some area. But not one of them gives any hope for added wisdom. Only Your Word offers that. Thank You for providing the means to know You more fully and to live life more abundantly.

SUNDAY, October 13

MONDAY, October 14 *Columbus Day*

TUESDAY, October 15

WEDNESDAY, October 16

THURSDAY, October 17

FRIDAY, October 18

SATURDAY, October 19

For the word of the L*ORD* *is right;*
and all his works are done in truth.

PSALM 33:4 KJV

Thank You, Lord, for the opportunity to live for You. I recognize the Holy Spirit's power at work in my life today. Just as I trusted Jesus to begin my new life by faith, I choose to live each day trusting Him. Guide me in all I do, as I submit to Your will. I desire to live my life in the flow of Your blessing. I seek to learn more each day as I grow in understanding and wisdom.

SUNDAY, October 20

MONDAY, October 21

TUESDAY, October 22

WEDNESDAY, October 23

THURSDAY, October 24

FRIDAY, October 25

SATURDAY, October 26

In the same way you received Jesus our Lord and Messiah by faith, continue your journey of faith, progressing further into your union with him! Your spiritual roots go deeply into his life as you are continually infused with strength, encouraged in every way.

COLOSSIANS 2:6–7 TPT

Heavenly Father, Your Word is limitless and unbreakable. Thank You, God, for giving me Your Word—Your promises for all eternity. You cannot lie. You say it, and it is so. I choose to trust and believe Your Word above all else. I will grow in faith and stand firm on You and the power of Your Word.

SUNDAY, October 27

MONDAY, October 28

TUESDAY, October 29

WEDNESDAY, October 30

THURSDAY, October 31

Halloween

FRIDAY, November 1

SATURDAY, November 2

But Jesus looked at them and said to them, "With men this is impossible, but with God all things are possible."

MATTHEW 19:26 NKJV

NOVEMBER 2024

SUNDAY	MONDAY	TUESDAY	WEDNESDAY
27	28	29	30
3 *Daylight Saving Time Ends*	4	5 *Election Day*	6
10	11 *Veterans Day*	12	13
17	18	19	20
24	25	26	27

THURSDAY	FRIDAY	SATURDAY
31	1	2
7	8	9
14	15	16
21	22	23
28 *Thanksgiving Day*	29	30

OCTOBER

S	M	T	W	T	F	S
		1	2	3	4	5
6	7	8	9	10	11	12
13	14	15	16	17	18	19
20	21	22	23	24	25	26
27	28	29	30	31		

DECEMBER

S	M	T	W	T	F	S
1	2	3	4	5	6	7
8	9	10	11	12	13	14
15	16	17	18	19	20	21
22	23	24	25	26	27	28
29	30	31				

To See the Victory

Lord, sometimes it's hard to see the victory hidden in life's circumstances. As You hung on the cross, Your followers perceived it as a crushing defeat. They couldn't see what You could see. Even as You assured them, they couldn't see how Your death could bring victory. But once You rose again, they learned the eternal joy of having You with them always. Thank You for knowing the whole story. My victory is assured, and I will rejoice. I will see Your purpose and plan fulfilled in my life. You have made a way when I can't see it. So, I put my trust in You today. Help me rest in You.

GOALS *for this* MONTH

☐ ....

☐ ....

☐ ....

☐ ....

☐ ....

☐ ....

☐ ....

☐ ....

☐ ....

☐ ....

☐ ....

☐ ....

☐ ....

☐ ....

☐ ....

"You have sorrow now, but I will see you again and then you will rejoice; and no one can rob you of that joy."

JOHN 16:22 TLB

Heavenly Father, I will stay true to You. You have placed me on the right path. Nothing can take me out of Your hand. I am confident in Your truth. You have plans for me, and those plans are good. You knew me before I was born, and You planned my way. You walk with me and talk with me. When I ask, You answer. When I look to the right or to the left, You whisper gently, "This is the way to go. Follow Me."

SUNDAY, November 3 *Daylight Saving Time Ends*

MONDAY, November 4

TUESDAY, November 5 *Election Day*

WEDNESDAY, November 6

THURSDAY, November 7

FRIDAY, November 8

SATURDAY, November 9

You're blessed when you stay on course, walking steadily on the road revealed by God.

Psalm 119:1 MSG

Father, this morning I come before You and I praise You. You are good and loving. You have only my very best interests at heart. Take my hand and lead me. Show me the way to go. Like a child being carried in a loving parent's arms, let me relax and trust You. I know that You will never lead me astray. Thank You, God, for this assurance.

SUNDAY, November 10

MONDAY, November 11 *Veterans Day*

TUESDAY, November 12

WEDNESDAY, November 13

THURSDAY, November 14

FRIDAY, November 15

SATURDAY, November 16

Cause me to hear thy lovingkindness in the morning; for in thee do I trust: cause me to know the way wherein I should walk; for I lift up my soul unto thee.

PSALM 143:8 KJV

Mighty God, You are my hope. You have given me life and delivered me from death. I believe I will receive all that You have prepared for me. My life is Yours to command. I look to You for all the answers. When I don't yet see what You see, help my unbelief. Holy Spirit, please let me see what You see, and make me courageous enough to follow through with Your divine appointments.

SUNDAY, November 17

MONDAY, November 18

TUESDAY, November 19

WEDNESDAY, November 20

THURSDAY, November 21

FRIDAY, November 22

SATURDAY, November 23

But without faith it is impossible to please and be satisfactory to Him. For whoever would come near to God must [necessarily] believe that God exists and that He is the rewarder of those who earnestly and diligently seek Him [out].

HEBREWS 11:6 AMPC

Jesus, Your words in the Bible encourage me. I speak Your Word with my mouth, and hope rises in my heart. I will fight fear with faith, knowing Your glory and truth will overcome the darkness. No darkness can withstand even a sliver of light. I choose to walk in Your light each day.

SUNDAY, November 24

MONDAY, November 25

TUESDAY, November 26

WEDNESDAY, November 27

THURSDAY, November 28 *Thanksgiving Day*

FRIDAY, November 29

SATURDAY, November 30

Arise, shine; for your light has come!
And the glory of the LORD is risen upon you.
For behold, the darkness shall cover the
earth, and deep darkness the people;
but the LORD will arise over you, and
His glory will be seen upon you.

ISAIAH 60:1–2 NKJV

DECEMBER 2024

SUNDAY	MONDAY	TUESDAY	WEDNESDAY
1	2	3	4
8	9	10	11
15	16	17	18
22	23	24 *Christmas Eve*	25 *Christmas Day/ Hanukkah Begins at Sundown*
29	30	31 *New Year's Eve*	1

THURSDAY	FRIDAY	SATURDAY
5	6	7
12	13	14
19	20	21 *First Day of Winter*
26	27	28
2	3	4

NOVEMBER

S	M	T	W	T	F	S
					1	2
3	4	5	6	7	8	9
10	11	12	13	14	15	16
17	18	19	20	21	22	23
24	25	26	27	28	29	30

JANUARY

S	M	T	W	T	F	S
			1	2	3	4
5	6	7	8	9	10	11
12	13	14	15	16	17	18
19	20	21	22	23	24	25
26	27	28	29	30	31	

When I Worry

Father, sometimes I don't come to You with all my problems. I'm afraid that my everyday struggles may be insignificant compared to other things happening in the world. I try to deal with them on my own or seek out other comforts. These sometimes don't solve the issue, or they can solve the problem but leave me feeling exhausted.

Thank You, Lord, for reminding me that You care about the details of our lives. You ask us to come to You with every burden, big or small. When we cast our anxieties on You, we can find answers to our problems and peace for our hearts. Today I give all my worries to You. I choose to believe You care deeply and will do what is best for me and the ones I love. I will not focus anymore on the things I ask You to control.

GOALS *for this* MONTH

☐ ....

☐ ....

☐ ....

☐ ....

☐ ....

☐ ....

☐ ....

☐ ....

☐ ....

☐ ....

☐ ....

☐ ....

☐ ....

☐ ....

☐ ....

☐ ....

Cast all your anxiety on him
because he cares for you.

1 PETER 5:7 NIV

Thank You, Father, for doing miracles in my heart and in my life. Forgive me when I've doubted, and help me trust You more each day. When You speak to me and give me a promise, I will hold fast to it. I will believe You and encourage myself in Your Word. Even when the miracle looks like the smallest thing—such as a cloud the size of a man's fist—I will stand strong and see the rain poured out lavishly on my life.

SUNDAY, December 1

MONDAY, December 2

TUESDAY, December 3

WEDNESDAY, December 4

THURSDAY, December 5

FRIDAY, December 6

SATURDAY, December 7

You are the God who performs miracles.
You have made your strength
known among the nations.

PSALM 77:14 GW

Just as Jesus taught His disciples to pray, I ask You, God, to teach me to pray. Help me to make prayer a priority, to esteem my time with You and guard it as a precious opportunity. May You find me daily on my knees before You, where I receive the strength and the courage I need to face the challenges of this fallen world.

SUNDAY, December 8

MONDAY, December 9

TUESDAY, December 10

WEDNESDAY, December 11

THURSDAY, December 12

FRIDAY, December 13

SATURDAY, December 14

Once Jesus was praying in a certain place. When he stopped praying, one of his disciples said to him, "Lord, teach us to pray as John taught his disciples."

LUKE 11:1 GW

God, my life is in You. You alone are my rest. I find peace in Your presence. Thank You for Your all-surpassing strength. When I stumble, You hold me up. I refuse to be shaken by the challenges facing me. When I can't catch my breath, You pour oxygen into my soul. I will not be moved when things don't go my way. I will rise above the disappointment because my future is assured. Because of You, I am set for life.

SUNDAY, December 15

MONDAY, December 16

TUESDAY, December 17

WEDNESDAY, December 18

THURSDAY, December 19

FRIDAY, December 20

SATURDAY, December 21 *First Day of Winter*

God, the one and only—I'll wait as long as he says. Everything I hope for comes from him, so why not? He's solid rock under my feet, breathing room for my soul, an impregnable castle: I'm set for life.

PSALM 62:5–6 MSG

I come to You, Lord Jesus. That is the first step. I come before You now in this quiet moment. As I begin this new day, calm my spirit. There is work that must be done today. But even as I work, I can find rest in You. Ease the tension and stress in me, Lord, as only You can do. Thank You for a sense of peace.

SUNDAY, December 22

MONDAY, December 23

TUESDAY, December 24 *Christmas Eve*

WEDNESDAY, December 25

Christmas Day / Hanukkah Begins at Sundown

THURSDAY, December 26

FRIDAY, December 27

SATURDAY, December 28

Come unto me, all ye that labour and are heavy laden, and I will give you rest.

MATTHEW 11:28 KJV

JANUARY 2025

SUNDAY	MONDAY	TUESDAY	WEDNESDAY
29	30	31	1 *New Year's Day*
5	6	7	8
12	13	14	15
19	20 *Martin Luther King Jr. Day*	21	22
26	27	28	29

THURSDAY	FRIDAY	SATURDAY
2	3	4
9	10	11
16	17	18
23	24	25
30	31	1

DECEMBER

S	M	T	W	T	F	S
1	2	3	4	5	6	7
8	9	10	11	12	13	14
15	16	17	18	19	20	21
22	23	24	25	26	27	28
29	30	31				

FEBRUARY

S	M	T	W	T	F	S
						1
2	3	4	5	6	7	8
9	10	11	12	13	14	15
16	17	18	19	20	21	22
23	24	25	26	27	28	

Run to God!

Father, on hard days, help me not to grumble or fuss with You like a small child. Shut my mouth so I don't complain to others. I can be such a whiner! When I am angry, teach me to run *to* You instead of *away* from You. When I encounter difficulty or disappointment, remind me that I can never hide from You. When I feel scared, weak, or alone, hold me tight and don't let me go. Lift my heart and give me strength. Remind me of all You've done. Bring Your promises to life in me, and help me push through the hard places. I do love You with all my heart and soul. You are my strength in every circumstance—good or bad.

GOALS *for this* MONTH

- [ ]
- [ ]
- [ ]
- [ ]
- [ ]
- [ ]
- [ ]
- [ ]
- [ ]
- [ ]
- [ ]
- [ ]
- [ ]
- [ ]
- [ ]
- [ ]

The Lord is a strong fortress.
The godly run to him and are safe.

PROVERBS 18:10 TLB

Lord, You are always there, and You are consistently patient with me. What if it were not so? What if You reached Your limit and showed the wrath that I deserve in my sinful imperfection? Because of Your great patience with me, let me not grow tired of being patient myself. Let me model what You have shown me by Your example. Thank You for Your great patience with me, God.

SUNDAY, December 29

MONDAY, December 30

TUESDAY, December 31 *New Year's Eve*

WEDNESDAY, January 1

New Year's Day

THURSDAY, January 2

FRIDAY, January 3

SATURDAY, January 4

And let us not be weary in well doing: for in due season we shall reap, if we faint not.

GALATIANS 6:9 KJV

Thank You, Lord, for knocking on the door of my heart. Thank You for giving me the courage to answer and invite You into my life. Now I ask You to help me encourage others to answer that same knock on their heart's door. Help me pay attention when You bring people across my path who are ready for a seed of hope to be planted in their hearts. Give me Your words to speak into their lives.

SUNDAY, January 5

MONDAY, January 6

TUESDAY, January 7

WEDNESDAY, January 8

THURSDAY, January 9

FRIDAY, January 10

SATURDAY, January 11

Behold, I stand at the door and knock; if anyone hears and listens to and heeds My voice and opens the door, I will come in to him and will eat with him, and he [will eat] with Me.

REVELATION 3:20 AMPC

Father, I really have a lot to do, and I'm not very good at multitasking. I need Your help each day as I organize the chores that need to be done. Show me how to prioritize my workload so that I can get things done in the most efficient manner, and let my work be pleasing in Your sight.

SUNDAY, January 12

MONDAY, January 13

TUESDAY, January 14

WEDNESDAY, January 15

THURSDAY, January 16

FRIDAY, January 17

SATURDAY, January 18

But seek ye first the kingdom of God, and his righteousness; and all these things shall be added unto you.

MATTHEW 6:33 KJV

Lord, I refuse to quit! I'm holding on to hope. My hope is in You, my rock and my Redeemer. If I did quit, I realize I would just become stuck. The only way out is to put one foot in front of the other. Give me strength to endure this season. Eventually it will pass. I must keep pressing on, day after day. I will come out of this on the other side. I will look back and see just how far we've come together.

SUNDAY, January 19

MONDAY, January 20 *Martin Luther King Jr. Day*

TUESDAY, January 21

WEDNESDAY, January 22

THURSDAY, January 23

FRIDAY, January 24

SATURDAY, January 25

Wait, Israel, for God. Wait with hope. Hope now; hope always!

Psalm 131:3 MSG

Heavenly Father, thank You for the Bible. It is filled with everything I need to follow after You. Like a bright flashlight in the darkest of nights, it shows me the way forward toward the life You have for me. It guides me in wisdom, helping me see the stumbling blocks in my way so that I can navigate carefully over them without falling.

SUNDAY, January 26

MONDAY, January 27

TUESDAY, January 28

WEDNESDAY, January 29

THURSDAY, January 30

FRIDAY, January 31

SATURDAY, February 1

Truth's shining light guides me in my choices and decisions; the revelation of your Word makes my pathway clear.

PSALM 119:105 TPT

FEBRUARY 2025

SUNDAY	MONDAY	TUESDAY	WEDNESDAY
26	27	28	29
2	3	4	5
9	10	11	12
16	17 *Presidents' Day*	18	19
23	24	25	26

THURSDAY	FRIDAY	SATURDAY
30	31	1
6	7	8
13	14 *Valentine's Day*	15
20	21	22
27	28	1

JANUARY

S	M	T	W	T	F	S
			1	2	3	4
5	6	7	8	9	10	11
12	13	14	15	16	17	18
19	20	21	22	23	24	25
26	27	28	29	30	31	

MARCH

S	M	T	W	T	F	S
						1
2	3	4	5	6	7	8
9	10	11	12	13	14	15
16	17	18	19	20	21	22
23	24	25	26	27	28	29
30	31					

Miracles Every Day

Lord, You are the miracle maker. Forgive me when I miss the small, everyday miracles. Help me see everything You are doing, all that You provide in my life. Teach me to be grateful for every gift You give. I will rejoice for every breath I take and every provision You make. I know You do great things. I believe You can bring the dead back to life. You make a way when there seems to be no way. You keep me from harm. I celebrate You, Lord! Thank You for being at work in my life even now, in this very moment.

GOALS *for this* MONTH

- [ ]
- [ ]
- [ ]
- [ ]
- [ ]
- [ ]
- [ ]
- [ ]
- [ ]
- [ ]
- [ ]
- [ ]
- [ ]
- [ ]
- [ ]

Jesus turned around and, seeing her, He said, Take courage, daughter! Your faith has made you well. And at once the woman was restored to health.

MATTHEW 9:22 AMPC

Lord, You have always known everything there is to know about me. You realize every movement of my heart and soul, and You comprehend every thought before it ever enters my mind. You know every step I will take before my journey even begins. You've gone into my future to prepare my way. Thank You for Your hand of love on my life and for the blessings You impart to me. There is no one who loves me like You do.

SUNDAY, February 2

MONDAY, February 3

TUESDAY, February 4

WEDNESDAY, February 5

THURSDAY, February 6

FRIDAY, February 7

SATURDAY, February 8

You saw who you created me to be before I became me! Before I'd ever seen the light of day, the number of days you planned for me were already recorded in your book.

PSALM 139:16 TPT

Father, at times I worry too much about what others think of me. Even when I just have a minor disagreement with a friend or coworker, I am afraid that the person will not like me anymore. I worry that I have not lived up to what was expected of me. Remind me, Father, that I must seek my ultimate strength and encouragement from You and You alone.

SUNDAY, February 9

MONDAY, February 10

TUESDAY, February 11

WEDNESDAY, February 12

THURSDAY, February 13

FRIDAY, February 14 *Valentine's Day*

SATURDAY, February 15

And David was greatly distressed; for the people spake of stoning him, because the soul of all the people was grieved, every man for his sons and for his daughters: but David encouraged himself in the LORD his God.

1 SAMUEL 30:6 KJV

Lord, You make all things beautiful in their time. My life looks so different today from the way it did before I met You. I know You are working on me. Sometimes it's hard to escape the pain. Tears cloud my vision, and I struggle to find my way. But I know You are making me new. I won't give up hope because Your promises are true. Even though I can't see it now, You have a plan to use me in wonderful ways. I give my all to You.

SUNDAY, February 16

MONDAY, February 17 *Presidents' Day*

TUESDAY, February 18

WEDNESDAY, February 19

THURSDAY, February 20

FRIDAY, February 21

SATURDAY, February 22

He has made everything beautiful in its time.
Also He has put eternity in their hearts,
except that no one can find out the work
that God does from beginning to end.

ECCLESIASTES 3:11 NKJV

God, Your Word says that You have given me a spirit of power, love, and a sound mind instead of fear. No matter how hard the season or how dark the night, fear has no place in my life. It will not conquer me because You defeated fear for me. I stay close to You, always in Your presence. You are my strength and my peace. Your comfort surrounds me. Your perfect love casts away all fear.

SUNDAY, February 23

MONDAY, February 24

TUESDAY, February 25

WEDNESDAY, February 26

THURSDAY, February 27

FRIDAY, February 28

SATURDAY, March 1

Even when your path takes me through the valley of deepest darkness, fear will never conquer me. . . . Your authority is my strength and my peace. The comfort of your love takes away my fear. I'll never be lonely, for you are near.

PSALM 23:4 TPT

MARCH 2025

SUNDAY	MONDAY	TUESDAY	WEDNESDAY
23	24	25	26
2	3	4	5 *Ash Wednesday*
9 *Daylight Saving Time Begins*	10	11	12
16	17 *St. Patrick's Day*	18	19
23 / 30	24 / 31	25	26

THURSDAY	FRIDAY	SATURDAY
27	28	1
6	7	8
13	14	15
20 *First Day of Spring*	21	22
27	28	29

FEBRUARY

S	M	T	W	T	F	S
						1
2	3	4	5	6	7	8
9	10	11	12	13	14	15
16	17	18	19	20	21	22
23	24	25	26	27	28	

APRIL

S	M	T	W	T	F	S
		1	2	3	4	5
6	7	8	9	10	11	12
13	14	15	16	17	18	19
20	21	22	23	24	25	26
27	28	29	30			

Say and Do Good

Lord, my words really matter. What I say about myself and about others is important. My words lead to actions, and my actions demonstrate the fruit growing in my life. I want to please You and produce good fruit for others to see—the kind of fruit that points them to You. Please place a guard over my mouth. Help me think about the words I say before I speak them. I want my words and actions to bring blessing and life into my life and into the lives of others. May I be an encourager who offers hope in all I say and do.

GOALS *for this* MONTH

☐ ....

☐ ....

☐ ....

☐ ....

☐ ....

☐ ....

☐ ....

☐ ....

☐ ....

☐ ....

☐ ....

☐ ....

☐ ....

☐ ....

God our Father loved us and by his kindness gave us everlasting encouragement and good hope. Together with our Lord Jesus Christ, may he encourage and strengthen you to do and say everything that is good.

2 THESSALONIANS 2:16–17 GW

Deadlines, sports schedules, unexpected overnight company—I'm about to pull out my hair! I know we all have our share of stress, but didn't I get an extra load this week, Father? I'm not sure what the purpose of it is, but I know there's a reason. Lord, give me patience through the ordeal, and let me please You.

SUNDAY, March 2

MONDAY, March 3

TUESDAY, March 4

WEDNESDAY, March 5 *Ash Wednesday*

THURSDAY, March 6

FRIDAY, March 7

SATURDAY, March 8

Take my yoke upon you, and learn of me; for I am meek and lowly in heart: and ye shall find rest unto your souls. For my yoke is easy, and my burden is light.

MATTHEW 11:29–30 KJV

I trust You, Lord. I am learning every day that no one else could ever love me like You do. I look at true human love in my life, and I realize Your love is beyond measure. No matter what comes my way, nothing can remove me from Your hand. Your unconditional, all-consuming love is powerful. It gives me the strength I need to step out in faith, to believe what others perceive as unbelievable.

SUNDAY, March 9 *Daylight Saving Time Begins*

MONDAY, March 10

TUESDAY, March 11

WEDNESDAY, March 12

THURSDAY, March 13

FRIDAY, March 14

SATURDAY, March 15

For I am persuaded that neither death nor life, nor angels nor principalities nor powers, nor things present nor things to come, nor height nor depth, nor any other created thing, shall be able to separate us from the love of God which is in Christ Jesus our Lord.

ROMANS 8:38–39 NKJV

God, it is hard for me to accept that coming to You in my need and hurt is a sign of weakness. But my strength comes from only You and not from me. While I try to fix my feelings on my own, You offer acceptance and forgiveness. I will rest in that truth today. I am forgiven!

SUNDAY, March 16

MONDAY, March 17 — *St. Patrick's Day*

TUESDAY, March 18

WEDNESDAY, March 19

THURSDAY, March 20 *First Day of Spring*

FRIDAY, March 21

SATURDAY, March 22

Godly sorrow brings repentance that leads to salvation and leaves no regret, but worldly sorrow brings death.

2 CORINTHIANS 7:10 NIV

New seasons can be exciting, Father, but they're not without challenges. I want to be excited about what You are going to do. I will not camp out on past failures or things I wish could have stayed the same. You have a purpose to every season. I am waiting and watching. I am expecting the new. I believe it will be a glorious surprise.

SUNDAY, March 23

MONDAY, March 24

TUESDAY, March 25

WEDNESDAY, March 26

THURSDAY, March 27

FRIDAY, March 28

SATURDAY, March 29

Do not [earnestly] remember the former things; neither consider the things of old. Behold, I am doing a new thing! Now it springs forth; do you not perceive and know it and will you not give heed to it? I will even make a way in the wilderness and rivers in the desert.

ISAIAH 43:18–19 AMPC

APRIL 2025

SUNDAY	MONDAY	TUESDAY	WEDNESDAY
30	31	1	2
6	7	8	9
13 *Palm Sunday*	14	15	16
20 *Easter Sunday*	21	22	23
27	28	29	30

THURSDAY	FRIDAY	SATURDAY
3	4	5
10	11	12 *Passover Begins at Sundown*
17	18 *Good Friday*	19
24	25	26
1	2	3

MARCH

S	M	T	W	T	F	S
						1
2	3	4	5	6	7	8
9	10	11	12	13	14	15
16	17	18	19	20	21	22
23	24	25	26	27	28	29
30	31					

MAY

S	M	T	W	T	F	S
				1	2	3
4	5	6	7	8	9	10
11	12	13	14	15	16	17
18	19	20	21	22	23	24
25	26	27	28	29	30	31

Refuse to Quit

Lord, sometimes I want to say, “Beam me up, God!” I want to escape this place, with all its troubles and temptations. But You have given me life and definite purpose. I know You have work for me to do here. You know my passion. You created me with a uniqueness. I can do something no one else can do. I can touch lives perhaps no one else can touch for You. Let me help the hungry, the oppressed, the imprisoned, the homeless, and the wounded. Show me the plans You have for me. Give me strength for today. I refuse to quit! I will do all that You’ve asked me to do.

GOALS *for this* MONTH

- [ ]
- [ ]
- [ ]
- [ ]
- [ ]
- [ ]
- [ ]
- [ ]
- [ ]
- [ ]
- [ ]
- [ ]
- [ ]
- [ ]
- [ ]

"But take courage, O Zerubbabel and Joshua and all the people; take courage and work, for I am with you, says the Lord Almighty."

HAGGAI 2:4 TLB

God, sometimes negative thoughts consume me. I want to think Your thoughts for me, for my life, and for my future. I want to take my negative thoughts and turn them around so that they become positive, faith-filled affirmations. I will pay more attention to what I'm thinking. I choose to think on the truth, the reputable, honorable things.

SUNDAY, March 30

MONDAY, March 31

TUESDAY, April 1

WEDNESDAY, April 2

THURSDAY, April 3

FRIDAY, April 4

SATURDAY, April 5

Whatever things are true, whatever things are noble, whatever things are just, whatever things are pure, whatever things are lovely, whatever things are of good report. . . meditate on these things.

PHILIPPIANS 4:8 NKJV

Heavenly Father, I come to You first. I will overcome this world, just as Jesus did, through prayer. Help me remember that I don't have to do this life alone. You are with me—helping me, guiding me, protecting me, and cheering me on.

SUNDAY, April 6

MONDAY, April 7

TUESDAY, April 8

WEDNESDAY, April 9

THURSDAY, April 10

FRIDAY, April 11

SATURDAY, April 12

Passover Begins at Sundown

Shall I look to the mountain gods for help?
No! My help is from Jehovah who made
the mountains! And the heavens too!

PSALM 121:1–2 TLB

Lord, You are my peace. I can't find peace in anyone or anything else. This world is full of chaos, and it does its best to crowd into my space. But You are my rock, my confidence. I can step away from the race happening in this world. I can sit down in the quiet of Your presence and experience great peace—Your peace, not my own.

SUNDAY, April 13 *Palm Sunday*

MONDAY, April 14

TUESDAY, April 15

WEDNESDAY, April 16

THURSDAY, April 17

FRIDAY, April 18 *Good Friday*

SATURDAY, April 19

Until at last the Spirit is poured down on us from heaven. Then once again enormous crops will come. Then justice will rule through all the land, and out of justice, peace. Quietness and confidence will reign forever more.

ISAIAH 32:15–17 TLB

I am created for relationship with You, Lord. Remind me daily that You desire face time with me. Just as You walked in the garden with Adam and talked with him, You desire that same fellowship with me. I will take time for You. I will not allow the busyness of life to overcrowd us.

SUNDAY, April 20 *Easter Sunday*

MONDAY, April 21

TUESDAY, April 22

WEDNESDAY, April 23

THURSDAY, April 24

FRIDAY, April 25

SATURDAY, April 26

The L*ORD* *would speak to Moses face to face, as one speaks to a friend.*

EXODUS 33:11 NIV

God, You have rescued me from the power of darkness and brought me into the kingdom of Your Son. Jesus paid the ultimate price to free me, and my sins are forgiven. Because of His great sacrifice, I am no longer separated from You. I can walk into Your presence without sin, fault, or blame.

SUNDAY, April 27

MONDAY, April 28

TUESDAY, April 29

WEDNESDAY, April 30

THURSDAY, May 1 *National Day of Prayer*

FRIDAY, May 2

SATURDAY, May 3

He is the image of the invisible God, the firstborn of all creation. . . . He existed before everything and holds everything together.

COLOSSIANS 1:15, 17 GW

MAY 2025

SUNDAY	MONDAY	TUESDAY	WEDNESDAY
27	28	29	30
4	5	6	7
11 *Mother's Day*	12	13	14
18	19	20	21
25	26 *Memorial Day*	27	28

THURSDAY	FRIDAY	SATURDAY
1 *National Day of Prayer*	2	3
8	9	10
15	16	17
22	23	24
29	30	31

APRII

S	M	T	W	T	F	S
		1	2	3	4	5
6	7	8	9	10	11	12
13	14	15	16	17	18	19
20	21	22	23	24	25	26
27	28	29	30			

JUNE

S	M	T	W	T	F	S
1	2	3	4	5	6	7
8	9	10	11	12	13	14
15	16	17	18	19	20	21
22	23	24	25	26	27	28
29	30					

Spread God's Peace

Dear God, I pray for peace throughout the world, where there's so much pain, destruction, and disregard for Your creation. Some say peace is impossible—but with You all things are possible! Jesus declared peace for all Your children. We can never look to the world for true peace. That only comes from You. And although peace does not reign throughout the earth, it can reign in my heart. I can be a comfort to others in the middle of life's storms. Give me courage to speak life when things look dark. May Your peace be a tangible gift that I can share with others.

GOALS *for this* MONTH

- [ ]
- [ ]
- [ ]
- [ ]
- [ ]
- [ ]
- [ ]
- [ ]
- [ ]
- [ ]
- [ ]
- [ ]
- [ ]
- [ ]
- [ ]

"Peace I leave with you, My peace I give to you; not as the world gives do I give to you. Let not your heart be troubled, neither let it be afraid."

JOHN 14:27 NKJV

Most of the time I'm not very good at doing nothing. Even when I put my feet up, my mind races with thoughts of what I could or should be doing. I need calm inactivity. I know I don't make it a priority like I should. But today I accept Your invitation, God, to experience a deeper intimacy with You through times of rest.

SUNDAY, May 4

MONDAY, May 5

TUESDAY, May 6

WEDNESDAY, May 7

THURSDAY, May 8

FRIDAY, May 9

SATURDAY, May 10

When the Lord has given you rest from your sorrow and pain and from your trouble and unrest and from the hard service with which you were made to serve. . . . The whole earth is at rest and is quiet; they break forth into singing.

Isaiah 14:3, 7 AMPC

Father, You know the storms in my life, past and present. You know the one storm weighing heavily on my mind right now. The storm often feels stronger, more powerful, at night. My mind is flooded with negative thoughts pouring in like ocean water that threatens to sink a ship. But You, my God, are my peace and my calm in the storm. I turn my face to You.

SUNDAY, May 11 *Mother's Day*

MONDAY, May 12

TUESDAY, May 13

WEDNESDAY, May 14

THURSDAY, May 15

FRIDAY, May 16

SATURDAY, May 17

Let the morning bring me word of your unfailing love, for I have put my trust in you.

PSALM 143:8 NIV

Dear God, I'm a far cry from perfect, but I'm confident in the knowledge that You love me just as I am. You are the one who has begun a work in me, and You will be faithful to complete what has been started. What a thrill to know that You'll make me what You want me to be.

SUNDAY, May 18

MONDAY, May 19

TUESDAY, May 20

WEDNESDAY, May 21

THURSDAY, May 22

FRIDAY, May 23

SATURDAY, May 24

Let not mercy and truth forsake thee: bind them about thy neck; write them upon the table of thine heart.

PROVERBS 3:3 KJV

Why is it so hard to trust You sometimes, Lord? You have never failed me, and yet I struggle. I want to be full of faith. I want to accept every promise You make and believe they will happen for me, but sometimes I fear. Help me trust You. Help me have great faith. Today, I let go of my doubt. I surrender fully to You. Whatever is before me, I am determined to trust Your Word.

SUNDAY, May 25

MONDAY, May 26 *Memorial Day*

TUESDAY, May 27

WEDNESDAY, May 28

THURSDAY, May 29

FRIDAY, May 30

SATURDAY, May 31

Jesus marveled at this. He turned around and said to the crowd who had followed him, "Listen, everyone! Never have I found among the people of God a man like this who believes so strongly in me."

LUKE 7:9 TPT

JUNE 2025

SUNDAY	MONDAY	TUESDAY	WEDNESDAY
1	2	3	4
8	9	10	11
15 *Father's Day*	16	17	18
22	23	24	25
29	30	1	2

THURSDAY	FRIDAY	SATURDAY
5	6	7
12	13	14 *Flag Day*
19	20 *First Day of Summer*	21
26	27	28
3	4	5

MAY

S	M	T	W	T	F	S
				1	2	3
4	5	6	7	8	9	10
11	12	13	14	15	16	17
18	19	20	21	22	23	24
25	26	27	28	29	30	31

JULY

S	M	T	W	T	F	S
		1	2	3	4	5
6	7	8	9	10	11	12
13	14	15	16	17	18	19
20	21	22	23	24	25	26
27	28	29	30	31		

When I Need Strength

Father, I come to You today and ask for strength. I'm done relying on myself and placing my problems on others. I choose to step out of sadness and hurt into the joy only You give. From this joy comes the strength to finish my day and to get out of bed tomorrow. I can't find that anywhere else but in Your presence.

Your daughters don't have to carry the stress of life alone. You give me the gift of the Holy Spirit. You ask me to come to You with all my burdens and doubts and promise to take these on Yourself. Thank You for that today. When I share my load with You, I can be more willing and open to do other tasks set before me.

GOALS *for this* MONTH

- [ ] ....
- [ ] ....
- [ ] ....
- [ ] ....
- [ ] ....
- [ ] ....
- [ ] ....
- [ ] ....
- [ ] ....
- [ ] ....
- [ ] ....
- [ ] ....
- [ ] ....
- [ ] ....
- [ ] ....
- [ ] ....

"Do not grieve, for the joy of the LORD is your strength."

NEHEMIAH 8:10 NIV

God, forgive me for my unbelief. Sometimes circumstances surround me and I am tempted to think You've forgotten me. But You would never abandon me. I remember the many times before when You rescued me. You showed up and delivered me. You've promised to do amazing things in my life. I am ready for a "suddenly"—a big surprise that will amaze me. I believe You will do abundantly above all I can ask or think.

SUNDAY, June 1

MONDAY, June 2

TUESDAY, June 3

WEDNESDAY, June 4

THURSDAY, June 5

FRIDAY, June 6

SATURDAY, June 7

"Look at the nations and watch—and be utterly amazed. For I am going to do something in your days that you would not believe, even if you were told."

HABAKKUK 1:5 NIV

Lord, help me hold on tight to You. Let Your ways be made known to me. May they sink deeply into my understanding. It's not enough to hear Your desires for my life; I must focus my thoughts, my will, and my emotions in the right direction. Sometimes paying attention is hard work. I tune my spiritual ears to Your Word today. I will not just hear You but will also obey Your truths.

SUNDAY, June 8

MONDAY, June 9

TUESDAY, June 10

WEDNESDAY, June 11

THURSDAY, June 12

FRIDAY, June 13

SATURDAY, June 14 *Flag Day*

This is why it is so crucial that we be all the more engaged and attentive to the truths that we have heard so that we do not drift off course.

HEBREWS 2:1 TPT

God, I refuse to give up! I've been waiting, pressing in, asking and trusting that everything You've promised will occur. Thank You for the joy and the strength You've given me to endure this season. Thank You for the small things that are bringing about Your purpose and plans. I agree with Your Word. All that You've promised is on its way.

SUNDAY, June 15 *Father's Day*

MONDAY, June 16

TUESDAY, June 17

WEDNESDAY, June 18

THURSDAY, June 19

FRIDAY, June 20

First Day of Summer

SATURDAY, June 21

"Things are going to happen so fast your head will swim, one thing fast on the heels of the other. You won't be able to keep up. Everything will be happening at once— and everywhere you look, blessings! Blessings like wine pouring off the mountains and hills."

AMOS 9:13 MSG

Lord, You created me. You know my history and my future. You placed me on this earth to live a life pleasing to You, to know You and to serve You. No one else knows me like You do. I am grateful to be a part of Your family. I am thankful for all You've done in my life. I never have to wonder where I belong. I belong to You.

SUNDAY, June 22

MONDAY, June 23

TUESDAY, June 24

WEDNESDAY, June 25

THURSDAY, June 26

FRIDAY, June 27

SATURDAY, June 28

"Don't you realize that God was speaking directly to you when he said, 'I am the God of Abraham, Isaac, and Jacob'? So God is not the God of the dead, but of the living."

MATTHEW 22:31–32 TLB

JULY 2025

SUNDAY	MONDAY	TUESDAY	WEDNESDAY
29	30	1	2
6	7	8	9
13	14	15	16
20	21	22	23
27	28	29	30

THURSDAY	FRIDAY	SATURDAY
3	4 *Independence Day*	5
10	11	12
17	18	19
24	25	26
31	1	2

JUNE

S	M	T	W	T	F	S
1	2	3	4	5	6	7
8	9	10	11	12	13	14
15	16	17	18	19	20	21
22	23	24	25	26	27	28
29	30					

AUGUST

S	M	T	W	T	F	S
					1	2
3	4	5	6	7	8	9
10	11	12	13	14	15	16
17	18	19	20	21	22	23
24	25	26	27	28	29	30
31						

Perfecting Every Concern

Father, You know the weight I carry in my mind. You know all my thoughts. Help me rise above the thoughts that pervade my mind and influence my heart. Your mercy and love for me endure forever. They will never run out. You are at work in my life perfecting every single concern I have. You work all things out for my good. I turn my eyes to Your Word. I will put Your Word in my heart and trust You, that every word, every promise You have made, will occur at the exact time You've purposed. I wait with patience.

GOALS *for this* MONTH

- [ ]
- [ ]
- [ ]
- [ ]
- [ ]
- [ ]
- [ ]
- [ ]
- [ ]
- [ ]
- [ ]
- [ ]
- [ ]
- [ ]
- [ ]

The LORD will perfect that which concerns me; Your mercy, O LORD, endures forever; do not forsake the works of Your hands.

PSALM 138:8 NKJV

God, I want to be a Proverbs 31 woman. My focus should not be on external beauty or the clothing and jewelry that I wear. Rather, may others notice my heart that is forever seeking You. I want nothing more than to be known as a woman of God. Protect me from vanity. Outward beauty is not lasting, but a beautiful spirit is. I meditate upon Your Word now, Lord. I want to honor You.

SUNDAY, June 29

MONDAY, June 30

TUESDAY, July 1

WEDNESDAY, July 2

THURSDAY, July 3

FRIDAY, July 4 *Independence Day*

SATURDAY, July 5

Favour is deceitful, and beauty is vain: but a woman that feareth the L*ORD, she shall be praised.*

PROVERBS 31:30 KJV

God, I want to make all my decisions according to Your will. Above all, I want to follow where You lead in my life. I need Your wisdom. I have a hard decision to make. It's difficult because there seems to be no solution that won't hurt someone. Help me find the path that You want me to go on—even if it's the rockiest one. Prepare the hearts of those I need to speak with so that what You give me to say is received in the best possible way.

SUNDAY, July 6

MONDAY, July 7

TUESDAY, July 8

WEDNESDAY, July 9

THURSDAY, July 10

FRIDAY, July 11

SATURDAY, July 12

I will praise and give thanks to You with uprightness of heart when I learn [by sanctified experiences] Your righteous judgments [Your decisions against and punishments for particular lines of thought and conduct].

PSALM 119:7 AMPC

Thank You, Jesus, for my salvation. I never have to worry about whether I am really a Christian. No one can ever convince me otherwise. The same Spirit that raised You from the dead resides in me. That power is available to me, and I lean into it.

SUNDAY, July 13

MONDAY, July 14

TUESDAY, July 15

WEDNESDAY, July 16

THURSDAY, July 17

FRIDAY, July 18

SATURDAY, July 19

And if the Spirit of him who raised Jesus from the dead is living in you, he who raised Christ from the dead will also give life to your mortal bodies because of his Spirit who lives in you.

ROMANS 8:11 NIV

My life is a song of praise to You, my faithful Father, the giver of life! When people hear my testimony of Your goodness, may they come to know You. I want others to notice the difference in me and wonder why I have such joy, such peace. May I point them to You, Lord, and may they trust in You for salvation.

SUNDAY, July 20

MONDAY, July 21

TUESDAY, July 22

WEDNESDAY, July 23

THURSDAY, July 24

FRIDAY, July 25

SATURDAY, July 26

And he hath put a new song in my mouth, even praise unto our God: many shall see it, and fear, and shall trust in the LORD*.*

PSALM 40:3 KJV

Heavenly Father, I want to let my light—the life that comes from You—shine before everyone. Create in me a clean heart, and cleanse me from all selfishness. My life will only shine if You are the source. I don't want to just get by, living a casual Christian life. I want my life to make a difference. Teach me to live and act in a way that speaks Your truth to others. Fill me with an undying passion to see lives changed for Your glory.

SUNDAY, July 27

MONDAY, July 28

TUESDAY, July 29

WEDNESDAY, July 30

THURSDAY, July 31

FRIDAY, August 1

SATURDAY, August 2

Light exposes the true character of everything because light makes everything easy to see. That's why it says: "Wake up, sleeper! Rise from the dead, and Christ will shine on you."

EPHESIANS 5:13–14 GW

AUGUST 2025

SUNDAY	MONDAY	TUESDAY	WEDNESDAY
27	28	29	30
3	4	5	6
10	11	12	13
17	18	19	20
24 / 31	25	26	27

THURSDAY	FRIDAY	SATURDAY
31	1	2
7	8	9
14	15	16
21	22	23
28	29	30

JULY

S	M	T	W	T	F	S
		1	2	3	4	5
6	7	8	9	10	11	12
13	14	15	16	17	18	19
20	21	22	23	24	25	26
27	28	29	30	31		

SEPTEMBER

S	M	T	W	T	F	S
	1	2	3	4	5	6
7	8	9	10	11	12	13
14	15	16	17	18	19	20
21	22	23	24	25	26	27
28	29	30				

All Hope in Him

Today I place all my hope in You, God. I am learning that true peace can only come from You. I cannot depend on resting when a problem is resolved because often more problems are just around the corner. It does me no good to worry, so forgive me when I do. Help me stand firm in my confidence, knowing *You* are my hope. I am strong and courageous when I rest in Your holy hand. You work all things together for my good. Because of Your unfailing love, all power and authority belong to You. You have the final say regarding everything that concerns me. I will not let go of You. You are where my hope comes from.

GOALS *for this* MONTH

☐ ....

☐ ....

☐ ....

☐ ....

☐ ....

☐ ....

☐ ....

☐ ....

☐ ....

☐ ....

☐ ....

☐ ....

☐ ....

☐ ....

☐ ....

☐ ....

"Power belongs to you, God, and with you, Lord, is unfailing love."

PSALM 62:11–12 NIV

God, I am grateful to belong to You—to be Your child. Even more, I am thankful for my brothers and sisters in Christ that You have brought into my life. May I be a voice of encouragement to each of them. May Your words be my words when I speak into their lives as You inspire me to do so. May I speak with Your love, mercy, and grace.

SUNDAY, August 3

MONDAY, August 4

TUESDAY, August 5

WEDNESDAY, August 6

THURSDAY, August 7

FRIDAY, August 8

SATURDAY, August 9

It is the greatest joy of my life to hear that my children are consistently living their lives in the ways of truth!

3 JOHN 4 TPT

Father, waiting to live until my circumstances change is no way to live. I need to live now and enjoy the moments You've given me. I will live each day with thanksgiving and hope, knowing You are always at work; You are doing what is necessary to bring Your promises into my life at just the right time. *Now* is the right time to expect and experience Your saving grace, mercy, and love.

SUNDAY, August 10

MONDAY, August 11

TUESDAY, August 12

WEDNESDAY, August 13

THURSDAY, August 14

FRIDAY, August 15

SATURDAY, August 16

For he says, I listened to you at the time of my favor. And the day when you needed salvation, I came to your aid. So can't you see? Now is the time to respond to his favor! Now is the day of salvation!

2 CORINTHIANS 6:2 TPT

God, I look back at where I've been as I'm facing another trial, and I see that You've been faithful. As I trust You now, I know that You have a plan. You always bring me through. Help me not to grow tired. Honestly, sometimes I do want to give up. But then where would I be? I'd be stuck. I cannot quit. I must press on. You are my hope. You will deliver me from this hardship.

SUNDAY, August 17

MONDAY, August 18

TUESDAY, August 19

WEDNESDAY, August 20

THURSDAY, August 21

FRIDAY, August 22

SATURDAY, August 23

Consider it pure joy, my brothers and sisters, whenever you face trials of many kinds, because you know that the testing of your faith produces perseverance.

JAMES 1:2–3 NIV

God, when someone hurts me, I don't feel like blessing him or her. Remind me what Your Word teaches about love. Love keeps no record of wrongs. Love forgives. It restores. Love tries again. Love lets it go. Love blesses even when it's not my turn to bless! Give me a spirit of love that trumps evil. And allow me to bless those who hurt me. I can only do so in Your power.

SUNDAY, August 24

MONDAY, August 25

TUESDAY, August 26

WEDNESDAY, August 27

THURSDAY, August 28

FRIDAY, August 29

SATURDAY, August 30

Not rendering evil for evil, or railing for railing: but contrariwise blessing; knowing that ye are thereunto called, that ye should inherit a blessing.

1 PETER 3:9 KJV

SEPTEMBER 2025

SUNDAY	MONDAY	TUESDAY	WEDNESDAY
31	1 *Labor Day*	2	3
7	8	9	10
14	15	16	17
21	22 *First Day of Autumn*	23	24
28	29	30	1

THURSDAY	FRIDAY	SATURDAY
4	5	6
11	12	13
18	19	20
25	26	27
2	3	4

AUGUST

S	M	T	W	T	F	S
					1	2
3	4	5	6	7	8	9
10	11	12	13	14	15	16
17	18	19	20	21	22	23
24	25	26	27	28	29	30
31						

OCTOBER

S	M	T	W	T	F	S
			1	2	3	4
5	6	7	8	9	10	11
12	13	14	15	16	17	18
19	20	21	22	23	24	25
26	27	28	29	30	31	

Cheers to Giving

God, You are a generous giver. Your Word says You will provide seed to the sower and in due season I will reap a harvest. Thank You for the seed I've sown and for the harvest that is on the way. I realize what I have to give goes far beyond financial gifts. Open my eyes to any opportunity You set before me to give cheerfully. I appreciate each opportunity to be generous. Show me the many different ways You would have me give into the lives of others. Just as You meet all my needs, may I remain openhanded, ready to help others in every way I can.

GOALS *for this* MONTH

- [ ] ....
- [ ] ....
- [ ] ....
- [ ] ....
- [ ] ....
- [ ] ....
- [ ] ....
- [ ] ....
- [ ] ....
- [ ] ....
- [ ] ....
- [ ] ....
- [ ] ....
- [ ] ....

Each of you should give whatever you have decided. You shouldn't be sorry that you gave or feel forced to give, since God loves a cheerful giver.

2 CORINTHIANS 9:7 GW

Lord, each day that I have breath in my lungs is a gift from You. Forgive me for the times when my perspective has been on the problems I face. Help me make every minute count. Help me step back and enjoy the precious times You give me with You and with those I love. Give me a big-picture focus. Let me look deeply at the things that really matter and gloss over those that don't.

SUNDAY, August 31

MONDAY, September 1 *Labor Day*

TUESDAY, September 2

WEDNESDAY, September 3

THURSDAY, September 4

FRIDAY, September 5

SATURDAY, September 6

"Eye has not seen, nor ear heard, nor have entered into the heart of man the things which God has prepared for those who love Him." But God has revealed them to us through His Spirit. For the Spirit searches all things, yes, the deep things of God.

1 CORINTHIANS 2:9–10 NKJV

God, I know that You are my partner in this plan You have for me. Thank You for Your promise that all things work together for my good. Your plan is like a big puzzle, but I don't have a picture of what that puzzle looks like when it's finished. So as I put the pieces together, lead me through the work. I trust You to put the pieces in the right places so that when it is finished, my life looks exactly the way You have envisioned it.

SUNDAY, September 7

MONDAY, September 8

TUESDAY, September 9

WEDNESDAY, September 10

THURSDAY, September 11

FRIDAY, September 12

SATURDAY, September 13

We are assured and know that [God being a partner in their labor] all things work together and are [fitting into a plan] for good to and for those who love God and are called according to [His] design and purpose.

Romans 8:28 AMPC

Lord, everything good in my life comes from You. Often I forget to thank You. I am thankful for Your provision and Your protection. I am thankful for my family and friends. I am most of all thankful for the joy of my salvation, which comes through Christ. Give me a grateful heart, I pray.

SUNDAY, September 14

MONDAY, September 15

TUESDAY, September 16

WEDNESDAY, September 17

THURSDAY, September 18

FRIDAY, September 19

SATURDAY, September 20

And let the peace of God rule in your hearts, to the which also ye are called in one body; and be ye thankful.

COLOSSIANS 3:15 KJV

So many things have happened in my life that I don't understand. I've been angry, been frightened, and wanted answers. But today I choose to trust You, Lord. With all my heart I choose to acknowledge You. You know what You're doing. My life is in Your hands. I don't have to know why. I want the details, but if You decide I don't need them, then I submit to You.

SUNDAY, September 21

MONDAY, September 22 *First Day of Autumn*

TUESDAY, September 23

WEDNESDAY, September 24

THURSDAY, September 25

FRIDAY, September 26

SATURDAY, September 27

Trust in the L*ORD* *with all your heart and lean not on your own understanding; in all your ways submit to him, and he will make your paths straight.*

PROVERBS 3:5–6 NIV

OCTOBER 2025

SUNDAY	MONDAY	TUESDAY	WEDNESDAY
28	29	30	1
5	6	7	8
12	13 *Columbus Day*	14	15
19	20	21	22
26	27	28	29

THURSDAY	FRIDAY	SATURDAY
2	3	4
9	10	11
16	17	18
23	24	25
30	31 *Halloween*	1

SEPTEMBER

S	M	T	W	T	F	S
	1	2	3	4	5	6
7	8	9	10	11	12	13
14	15	16	17	18	19	20
21	22	23	24	25	26	27
28	29	30				

NOVEMBER

S	M	T	W	T	F	S
						1
2	3	4	5	6	7	8
9	10	11	12	13	14	15
16	17	18	19	20	21	22
23	24	25	26	27	28	29
30						

Confidence in Prayer

Father, thank You for Jesus. I know that because of faith in Him, I have access to the presence of God every second of the day. I am never alone. I know with complete trust that You'll answer my prayer. And I know that to pray confidently, I have to come to You with open hands and an open heart, willing to listen to what You have to say. Even if that includes something I don't want to hear.

I know that the key to confident prayer is praising Your name, confessing my sins, and aligning my will with Yours. When I pray, help me to recognize when I take my eyes off You. My first priority is following You and not my own desires. Thank You for being there.

GOALS *for this* MONTH

- [ ] ....
- [ ] ....
- [ ] ....
- [ ] ....
- [ ] ....
- [ ] ....
- [ ] ....
- [ ] ....
- [ ] ....
- [ ] ....
- [ ] ....
- [ ] ....
- [ ] ....
- [ ] ....

Let us draw near to God with a sincere heart and with the full assurance that faith brings, having our hearts sprinkled to cleanse us from a guilty conscience and having our bodies washed with pure water.

HEBREWS 10:22 NIV

Lord, I love You. You shield and defend me from the seen and the unseen. When circumstances suddenly go a different direction than I thought, I trust that You have prevented a more terrible thing from coming into my life. When I think I have no more strength for the struggle at hand, You become my strength. You are my defender and my deliverer. You pull me out of the mess. You are my salvation.

SUNDAY, September 28

MONDAY, September 29

TUESDAY, September 30

WEDNESDAY, October 1

THURSDAY, October 2

FRIDAY, October 3

SATURDAY, October 4

The Lord is my Rock, my Fortress, and my Deliverer; my God, my keen and firm Strength in Whom I will trust and take refuge, my Shield, and the Horn of my salvation, my High Tower.

PSALM 18:2 AMPC

How can I doubt my worth in Your eyes, Father? You know the number of hairs on my head. You created me, and You said that Your creation is very good. When I'm tempted to get down on myself, remind me that I am special to You, and there's no one just like me.

SUNDAY, October 5

MONDAY, October 6

TUESDAY, October 7

WEDNESDAY, October 8

THURSDAY, October 9

FRIDAY, October 10

SATURDAY, October 11

In the multitude of my thoughts within me thy comforts delight my soul.

PSALM 94:19 KJV

Lord, I am standing in the middle of transition. Many things that used to be are no longer so. It's time for me to lead myself and others in a forward motion. Although my responsibilities are changing, I am not without help. You've provided the training and preparation. I have all I need.

SUNDAY, October 12

MONDAY, October 13 *Columbus Day*

TUESDAY, October 14

WEDNESDAY, October 15

THURSDAY, October 16

FRIDAY, October 17

SATURDAY, October 18

Hold tightly to the pattern of truth I taught you, especially concerning the faith and love Christ Jesus offers you.

2 TIMOTHY 1:13 TLB

Heavenly Father, my salvation is a gift—something I could never earn, but a treasure given freely with no strings attached. It is mine and can never be taken from me. Nothing can separate me from Your love. Forgive me for the times that I doubted my salvation or thought it was something I needed to achieve or win. Thank You for believing in me, trusting me with Your love.

SUNDAY, October 19

MONDAY, October 20

TUESDAY, October 21

WEDNESDAY, October 22

THURSDAY, October 23

FRIDAY, October 24

SATURDAY, October 25

And by this we know that we are of the truth, and shall assure our hearts before Him. For if our heart condemns us, God is greater than our heart, and knows all things. Beloved, if our heart does not condemn us, we have confidence toward God.

1 JOHN 3:19–21 NKJV

Lord, You know my prayer requests before they ever cross my lips, and yet, I know You desire for me to ask. So today, I am asking You to perfect those things that weigh heavily on my heart and mind. I trust that You have already started working behind the scenes on my behalf. You know the details and how they should work out best for me.

SUNDAY, October 26

MONDAY, October 27

TUESDAY, October 28

WEDNESDAY, October 29

THURSDAY, October 30

FRIDAY, October 31 *Halloween*

SATURDAY, November 1

"The moment you began praying a command was given. I am here to tell you what it was, for God loves you very much. Listen and try to understand the meaning of the vision that you saw!"

DANIEL 9:23 TLB

NOVEMBER 2025

SUNDAY	MONDAY	TUESDAY	WEDNESDAY
26	27	28	29
2 *Daylight Saving Time Ends*	3	4 *Election Day*	5
9	10	11 *Veterans Day*	12
16	17	18	19
23 / 30	24	25	26

THURSDAY	FRIDAY	SATURDAY
30	31	1
6	7	8
13	14	15
20	21	22
27 *Thanksgiving Day*	28	29

OCTOBER

S	M	T	W	T	F	S
			1	2	3	4
5	6	7	8	9	10	11
12	13	14	15	16	17	18
19	20	21	22	23	24	25
26	27	28	29	30	31	

DECEMBER

S	M	T	W	T	F	S
	1	2	3	4	5	6
7	8	9	10	11	12	13
14	15	16	17	18	19	20
21	22	23	24	25	26	27
28	29	30	31			

Getting Older

Lord, I find myself reaching for what used to be. I tell myself that it was easier and better in my past and that age has only brought hardship. Why can't I go back to who I was? Where is that girl that trusted You so openly?

I know, Father, that You're the one who turns the seasons. I am where I am because You have found it important for me to be here. My age doesn't matter when I look at the eternity I get to spend with You.

I'm confident that every change to my body and circumstances has been ordained in Your will. I embrace the wisdom I have gained over the years, the scars and marks that led me closer to You. When I look at my life as a testament to You, I can embrace who I am.

GOALS *for this* MONTH

☐ ....

☐ ....

☐ ....

☐ ....

☐ ....

☐ ....

☐ ....

☐ ....

☐ ....

☐ ....

☐ ....

☐ ....

☐ ....

☐ ....

☐ ....

Do not say, "Why were the old days better than these?" For it is not wise to ask such questions.

ECCLESIASTES 7:10 NIV

Father God, when I'm tempted to allow my thoughts to pull me under the waters of anxiety, remind me that You never want me to be anxious about anything. I don't need to be worried. Today I spend time saturating my soul in prayer. Help me offer up faith-filled requests to You throughout the day. I will overflow with gratitude and thanksgiving.

SUNDAY, November 2 *Daylight Saving Time Ends*

MONDAY, November 3

TUESDAY, November 4 *Election Day*

WEDNESDAY, November 5

THURSDAY, November 6

FRIDAY, November 7

SATURDAY, November 8

Be anxious for nothing, but in everything by prayer and supplication, with thanksgiving, let your requests be made known to God.

PHILIPPIANS 4:6 NKJV

Heavenly Father, You have poured, are pouring, and will continue to pour out Your power in my life in astonishing ways. I am always ready for anything and everything. Because You prepare me, I am more than ready to do what needs to be done. Whatever I need, I can count on You to go above and beyond.

SUNDAY, November 9

MONDAY, November 10

TUESDAY, November 11 *Veterans Day*

WEDNESDAY, November 12

THURSDAY, November 13

FRIDAY, November 14

SATURDAY, November 15

And God is able to make all grace (every favor and earthly blessing) come to you in abundance, so that you may always and under all circumstances and whatever the need be self-sufficient.

2 CORINTHIANS 9:8 AMPC

Heavenly Father, because I am Your child, I am blessed. Pour out Your favor on me. Forgive me for the times You've prepared a blessing and I got in the way. Forgive me for trying to make things happen all by myself—in my timing instead of Yours. Give me ears to hear wisdom when You speak. I will listen to those You've placed in my life to mentor me. I choose to be pliable and moldable. I choose Your way and not my own.

SUNDAY, November 16

MONDAY, November 17

TUESDAY, November 18

WEDNESDAY, November 19

THURSDAY, November 20

FRIDAY, November 21

SATURDAY, November 22

And Esther obtained favor in the sight of all who saw her.

ESTHER 2:15 NKJV

Lord, I get lost in the busyness of life sometimes—a lot of the time—and forget that I am not of this world. My future is eternal. Help me remember what is important. Things of this life fade away when compared to eternity with You. Remind me to build up my treasure in heaven; this world is just a place I'm passing through.

SUNDAY, November 23

MONDAY, November 24

TUESDAY, November 25

WEDNESDAY, November 26

THURSDAY, November 27 *Thanksgiving Day*

FRIDAY, November 28

SATURDAY, November 29

"For here is the way God loved the world—
he gave his only, unique Son as a gift.
So now everyone who believes
in him will never perish but
experience everlasting life."

JOHN 3:16 TPT

DECEMBER 2025

SUNDAY	MONDAY	TUESDAY	WEDNESDAY
30	1	2	3
7	8	9	10
14 *Hanukkah Begins at Sundown*	15	16	17
21 *First Day of Winter*	22	23	24 *Christmas Eve*
28	29	30	31 *New Year's Eve*

THURSDAY	FRIDAY	SATURDAY
4	5	6
11	12	13
18	19	20
25 *Christmas Day*	26	27
1	2	3

NOVEMBER

S	M	T	W	T	F	S
						1
2	3	4	5	6	7	8
9	10	11	12	13	14	15
16	17	18	19	20	21	22
23	24	25	26	27	28	29
30						

JANUARY

S	M	T	W	T	F	S
				1	2	3
4	5	6	7	8	9	10
11	12	13	14	15	16	17
18	19	20	21	22	23	24
25	26	27	28	29	30	31

Listening to God's Direction

Father, thank You for Your wisdom. I've not always taken the time to ask You which way to go before moving forward, or even if I did ask, sometimes I didn't wait patiently for an answer. I desire Your will for my life. I want to be in the right place at the right time. May I move with You, forever listening for Your voice for direction. Show me the way I should go. Speak to me when I've gone off on my own. Bring me back to the place of peace—a place I can only find in You. Your ways are not my ways. Help me to always choose Your path for my life.

GOALS *for this* MONTH

- [ ] ....
- [ ] ....
- [ ] ....
- [ ] ....
- [ ] ....
- [ ] ....
- [ ] ....
- [ ] ....
- [ ] ....
- [ ] ....
- [ ] ....
- [ ] ....
- [ ] ....
- [ ] ....
- [ ] ....

Whether you turn to the right or to the left, your ears will hear a voice behind you, saying, "This is the way; walk in it."

ISAIAH 30:21 NIV

Jesus, You know my sorrow, my grief, my pain. No one truly understands my heart—but You. I have a lot of questions I want to know the answers to, and perhaps those answers can only come from You. Show me the path that is right, because sometimes I am blinded by my grief. Hold me tight as I let the tears fall. Wash away the brokenness.

SUNDAY, November 30

MONDAY, December 1

TUESDAY, December 2

WEDNESDAY, December 3

THURSDAY, December 4

FRIDAY, December 5

SATURDAY, December 6

Blessed be the God and Father of our Lord Jesus Christ, the Father of mercies and God of all comfort, who comforts us in all our tribulation, that we may be able to comfort those who are in any trouble, with the comfort with which we ourselves are comforted by God.

2 CORINTHIANS 1:3–4 NKJV

I find it difficult to even sit down to a meal, Father. Resting seems like such a far-fetched notion. I know You want me to find time to rest and spend time with You, but I'm on the go constantly, and I still don't get everything done. Please help me, Lord, to make resting a priority.

SUNDAY, December 7

MONDAY, December 8

TUESDAY, December 9

WEDNESDAY, December 10

THURSDAY, December 11

FRIDAY, December 12

SATURDAY, December 13

Cast thy burden upon the L*ORD, and he shall sustain thee: he shall never suffer the righteous to be moved.*

PSALM 55:22 KJV

Lord, I live in a messed-up world. When bad things happen to good people, it's difficult for me to understand. I know that You hold my life in Your hands. My time is not my own but Yours, and yet I desire a long life filled with Your goodness and love. Forgive me for the times I've closed off areas of my heart to You. I open them wide.

SUNDAY, December 14 *Hanukkah Begins at Sundown*

MONDAY, December 15

TUESDAY, December 16

WEDNESDAY, December 17

THURSDAY, December 18

FRIDAY, December 19

SATURDAY, December 20

Yes, Lord, help us against our enemies, for man's help is useless. With God's help we shall do mighty things, for he will trample down our foes.

PSALM 60:11–12 TLB

When the earth moves beneath me because of the circumstances of my life, I look to You, Lord. When hope threatens to escape me, You are the one I hold on to. You are my stability and strength. My heart will remain steady despite all I see. I turn my eyes to You. I look up because You are my light and my salvation.

SUNDAY, December 21 *First Day of Winter*

MONDAY, December 22

TUESDAY, December 23

WEDNESDAY, December 24 *Christmas Eve*

THURSDAY, December 25 *Christmas Day*

FRIDAY, December 26

SATURDAY, December 27

My heart will not fear even if an army rises to attack. I will not be shaken.

PSALM 27:3 TPT

God, I don't want to miss anything You have for me. I want to know You more. I want to go deeper in my relationship with You. Stir up Your life in me. Give me a desire for revitalization in my soul. Help me recognize distractions that keep me from reaching those goals You want me to reach.

SUNDAY, December 28

MONDAY, December 29

TUESDAY, December 30

WEDNESDAY, December 31 *New Year's Eve*

THURSDAY, January 1 *New Year's Day*

FRIDAY, January 2

SATURDAY, January 3

Revive us, and we will call upon Your name. Restore us, O Lord God of hosts; cause Your face to shine, and we shall be saved!

PSALM 80:18–19 NKJV

CONTACTS

Name:

Address:

Phone:

Email:

Name:

Address:

Phone:

Email:

Name:

Address:

Phone:

Email:

Name:

Address:

Phone:

Email:

Name:

Address:

Phone:

Email:

CONTACTS

Name:

Address:

Phone:

Email:

Name:

Address:

Phone:

Email:

Name:

Address:

Phone:

Email:

Name:

Address:

Phone:

Email:

Name:

Address:

Phone:

Email:

CONTACTS

Name:

Address:

Phone:

Email:

Name:

Address:

Phone:

Email:

Name:

Address:

Phone:

Email:

Name:

Address:

Phone:

Email:

Name:

Address:

Phone:

Email:

CONTACTS

Name:

Address:

Phone:

Email:

Name:

Address:

Phone:

Email:

Name:

Address:

Phone:

Email:

Name:

Address:

Phone:

Email:

Name:

Address:

Phone:

Email:

CONTACTS

Name:

Address:

Phone:

Email:

Name:

Address:

Phone:

Email:

Name:

Address:

Phone:

Email:

Name:

Address:

Phone:

Email:

Name:

Address:

Phone:

Email:

CONTACTS

Name:

Address:

Phone:

Email:

Name:

Address:

Phone:

Email:

Name:

Address:

Phone:

Email:

Name:

Address:

Phone:

Email:

Name:

Address:

Phone:

Email:

CONTACTS

Name:

Address:

Phone:

Email:

Name:

Address:

Phone:

Email:

Name:

Address:

Phone:

Email:

Name:

Address:

Phone:

Email:

Name:

Address:

Phone:

Email:

CONTACTS

Name:

Address:

Phone:

Email:

Name:

Address:

Phone:

Email:

Name:

Address:

Phone:

Email:

Name:

Address:

Phone:

Email:

Name:

Address:

Phone:

Email:

CONTACTS

Name:

Address:

Phone:

Email:

Name:

Address:

Phone:

Email:

Name:

Address:

Phone:

Email:

Name:

Address:

Phone:

Email:

Name:

Address:

Phone:

Email:

CONTACTS

Name:

Address:

Phone:

Email:

Name:

Address:

Phone:

Email:

Name:

Address:

Phone:

Email:

Name:

Address:

Phone:

Email:

Name:

Address:

Phone:

Email:

CONTACTS

Name:

Address:

Phone:

Email:

Name:

Address:

Phone:

Email:

Name:

Address:

Phone:

Email:

Name:

Address:

Phone:

Email:

Name:

Address:

Phone:

Email:

CONTACTS

Name:

Address:

Phone:

Email:

Name:

Address:

Phone:

Email:

Name:

Address:

Phone:

Email:

Name:

Address:

Phone:

Email:

Name:

Address:

Phone:

Email:

CONTACTS

Name:

Address:

Phone:

Email:

Name:

Address:

Phone:

Email:

Name:

Address:

Phone:

Email:

Name:

Address:

Phone:

Email:

Name:

Address:

Phone:

Email:

YEAR-*at*-*a*-GLANCE CALENDARS

2026

JANUARY

S	M	T	W	T	F	S
				1	2	3
4	5	6	7	8	9	10
11	12	13	14	15	16	17
18	19	20	21	22	23	24
25	26	27	28	29	30	31

FEBRUARY

S	M	T	W	T	F	S
1	2	3	4	5	6	7
8	9	10	11	12	13	14
15	16	17	18	19	20	21
22	23	24	25	26	27	28

MARCH

S	M	T	W	T	F	S
1	2	3	4	5	6	7
8	9	10	11	12	13	14
15	16	17	18	19	20	21
22	23	24	25	26	27	28
29	30	31				

APRIL

S	M	T	W	T	F	S
			1	2	3	4
5	6	7	8	9	10	11
12	13	14	15	16	17	18
19	20	21	22	23	24	25
26	27	28	29	30		

MAY

S	M	T	W	T	F	S
					1	2
3	4	5	6	7	8	9
10	11	12	13	14	15	16
17	18	19	20	21	22	23
24	25	26	27	28	29	30
31						

JUNE

S	M	T	W	T	F	S
	1	2	3	4	5	6
7	8	9	10	11	12	13
14	15	16	17	18	19	20
21	22	23	24	25	26	27
28	29	30				

JULY

S	M	T	W	T	F	S
			1	2	3	4
5	6	7	8	9	10	11
12	13	14	15	16	17	18
19	20	21	22	23	24	25
26	27	28	29	30	31	

AUGUST

S	M	T	W	T	F	S
						1
2	3	4	5	6	7	8
9	10	11	12	13	14	15
16	17	18	19	20	21	22
23	24	25	26	27	28	29
30	31					

SEPTEMBER

S	M	T	W	T	F	S
		1	2	3	4	5
6	7	8	9	10	11	12
13	14	15	16	17	18	19
20	21	22	23	24	25	26
27	28	29	30			

OCTOBER

S	M	T	W	T	F	S
				1	2	3
4	5	6	7	8	9	10
11	12	13	14	15	16	17
18	19	20	21	22	23	24
25	26	27	28	29	30	31

NOVEMBER

S	M	T	W	T	F	S
1	2	3	4	5	6	7
8	9	10	11	12	13	14
15	16	17	18	19	20	21
22	23	24	25	26	27	28
29	30					

DECEMBER

S	M	T	W	T	F	S
		1	2	3	4	5
6	7	8	9	10	11	12
13	14	15	16	17	18	19
20	21	22	23	24	25	26
27	28	29	30	31		

2027

JANUARY

S	M	T	W	T	F	S
					1	2
3	4	5	6	7	8	9
10	11	12	13	14	15	16
17	18	19	20	21	22	23
24	25	26	27	28	29	30
31						

FEBRUARY

S	M	T	W	T	F	S
	1	2	3	4	5	6
7	8	9	10	11	12	13
14	15	16	17	18	19	20
21	22	23	24	25	26	27
28						

MARCH

S	M	T	W	T	F	S
	1	2	3	4	5	6
7	8	9	10	11	12	13
14	15	16	17	18	19	20
21	22	23	24	25	26	27
28	29	30	31			

APRIL

S	M	T	W	T	F	S
				1	2	3
4	5	6	7	8	9	10
11	12	13	14	15	16	17
18	19	20	21	22	23	24
25	26	27	28	29	30	

MAY

S	M	T	W	T	F	S
						1
2	3	4	5	6	7	8
9	10	11	12	13	14	15
16	17	18	19	20	21	22
23	24	25	26	27	28	29
30	31					

JUNE

S	M	T	W	T	F	S
		1	2	3	4	5
6	7	8	9	10	11	12
13	14	15	16	17	18	19
20	21	22	23	24	25	26
27	28	29	30			

JULY

S	M	T	W	T	F	S
				1	2	3
4	5	6	7	8	9	10
11	12	13	14	15	16	17
18	19	20	21	22	23	24
25	26	27	28	29	30	31

AUGUST

S	M	T	W	T	F	S
1	2	3	4	5	6	7
8	9	10	11	12	13	14
15	16	17	18	19	20	21
22	23	24	25	26	27	28
29	30	31				

SEPTEMBER

S	M	T	W	T	F	S
			1	2	3	4
5	6	7	8	9	10	11
12	13	14	15	16	17	18
19	20	21	22	23	24	25
26	27	28	29	30		

OCTOBER

S	M	T	W	T	F	S
					1	2
3	4	5	6	7	8	9
10	11	12	13	14	15	16
17	18	19	20	21	22	23
24	25	26	27	28	29	30
31						

NOVEMBER

S	M	T	W	T	F	S
	1	2	3	4	5	6
7	8	9	10	11	12	13
14	15	16	17	18	19	20
21	22	23	24	25	26	27
28	29	30				

DECEMBER

S	M	T	W	T	F	S
			1	2	3	4
5	6	7	8	9	10	11
12	13	14	15	16	17	18
19	20	21	22	23	24	25
26	27	28	29	30	31	

CONTACTS

Name:

Address:

Phone:

Email:

Name:

Address:

Phone:

Email:

Name:

Address:

Phone:

Email:

Name:

Address:

Phone:

Email:

Name:

Address:

Phone:

Email: